MARCIA
CEBULSKA

NOW LET
ME FLY

Flint Hills Publishing

Now Let My Fly

Original Cover Art by Chris Millspaugh
www. chrismillspaugh.com

Cover Design by Amy Albright

stonypointgraphics.weebly.com

🌾Flint Hills Publishing
Topeka, Kansas
Tucson, Arizona
www.flinthillspublishing.com

Printed in the U.S.A.

Paperback Book: ISBN: 978-1-953583-86-4
Electronic Book ISBN: 978-1-953583-87-1

DEDICATION

_____

To the unsung heroes and heroines who, risking life and limb, turned their anger into action in pursuit of equality and justice.

Now Let Me Fly

(Traditional Spiritual)

I heard a rumbling in the sky

I thought the Lord was passing by

It was the good old chariot drawing nigh

Oh well, it shook the earth, swept the sky

Now let me fly

Oh, Lord, Lord ...

Now let me fly

INTRODUCTION

A Little Less "Mad" and a Little More "Do"

During the civil-rights struggle, Charles Hamilton Houston, Thurgood Marshall's law professor at Howard University, was known for preaching calm and strategy with his advice, "A little less 'mad' and a little more 'do.'" The plaintiffs in the five *Brown v. Board* cases all turned their "mad" into "do," benefiting the nation by crafting a more equitable society. At least on paper. At least legally.

Twenty-some years ago, I was awestruck by the stories of these ordinary citizens—barbers, taxi drivers, students, housewives, preachers, welders, moms—who stood up, who put their lives on the line, to help create a better, more perfect Union. Their stories were the inspiration for *Now Let Me Fly,* the play I was commissioned to write for the national celebration of *Brown v. Board*'s 50th anniversary in 2004.

Now, as we are approaching the 70th anniversary of the Supreme Court decision that overturned "separate but equal," I again feel the need to heed Charlie Houston's advice. Because I am, indeed "mad" at the state of things in our country in terms of racial justice. Because I, again, need the inspiration of those citizens who turned their anger into action. Who changed the law of the land. Who made a difference.

Citizens like Gardner Bishop, a barber on U Street in Washington, D.C. who organized the parents and children in his neighborhood where the Black school was not only separate, but crowded and ill-equipped. The only science equipment in the whole school was one Bunsen burner and a bowl of goldfish. Led by Bishop, 1,500 students went on strike.

1

An entourage of taxi cabs was organized to take the Black students from their ill-equipped high school to the half-empty brand-new fully equipped white school. That's some "do."

The school children in Farmville, Virginia also went on strike, but this time led by a fellow student, 16-year-old Barbara Rose Johns. She was a high school debater who had seen what white schools were like when she visited them with her debate team. They were not like the tar paper shacks where she attended classes. Inspired by her activist uncle, a fiery preacher named Vernon Johns, Barbara led her classmates to the courthouse and demanded better facilities. When the students didn't get results, they screwed up their courage and called the NAACP. Today, there is a museum at the R. R. Moton School, where I visited on a research trip. I walked the route from the school to the courthouse. I read the diary of the young girl who spoke out and led the strike. Before I started this work, I had never heard of Farmville, Virginia. This story of brave children had been buried. Our own children do not hear this story.

Or take the housewife in Delaware who wrote letters to the governor because her adopted daughter was passed every day by a school bus on its way up the hill. The school bus was headed toward the white school, next to the country club, complete with rosebushes and a baseball diamond. Meanwhile, her first grader, Shirley Barbara, had six busless miles to climb to a one-room schoolhouse with broken chairs and faulty plumbing. As Mrs. Bulah says in the play, "I see plenty of separates but not much equals."

When I started my research for this play, I read the oral histories archived at Washburn University School of Law. I learned stories of World War II soldiers who were guards over

Nazi prisoners of war but were not themselves allowed in the movie houses on base because they were Black. Fighting for freedom but not having it themselves, veterans became part of the movement.

In Clarendon County, South Carolina, Rev. Joseph DeLaine was both a minister and schoolteacher. Seeing firsthand how unequal the educational facilities were, he filed a suit to acquire buses for the Black children. But things turned violent and KKK Night Riders burned Rev. DeLaine's house to the ground.

Sarah Bulah, Oliver Brown, Rev. DeLaine, and the other plaintiffs were not just looking for a short route to school but human dignity. They were not alone. They were part of a movement. They were unsung heroes and heroines who need to be recognized.

And then, there were the lawyers. Charles Houston taught his students that "a lawyer who is not a social architect is a social parasite." In their work to attain equality for Black children, the Black attorneys for these cases ate at the back doors of restaurants, next to the garbage cans, because they weren't permitted inside. One night, Thurgood Marshall was led to a tall tree with a short rope. Lucky for all of us, his colleagues arrived in the nick of time and saved him.

Twenty years ago, the plaintiffs and the civil-rights attorneys for the *Brown v. Board* case inspired the writing of *Now Let Me Fly*. They still offer us inspiration and hope. Because of them, we can believe in the possibility of change, of group action, of a better future. Because of them and others like them, we can sit together, people of all skin shades, and enjoy a play.

Marcia Cebulska, Playwright

PLAY HISTORY

Now Let Me Fly was commissioned to celebrate the 50th anniversary of the *Brown v. Board of Education of Topeka* Supreme Court decision outlawing segregation in public education. The commission was underwritten by the Brown Foundation with generous funding from Washburn University. This volume is being published in commemoration of the 70th anniversary of the momentous *Brown v. Board* decision.

Now Let Me Fly premiered on May 17, 2004, at Topeka Performing Arts Center with contemporaneous reader's theatre performances at the National Constitution Center, the National Center for Civil Rights, Rothko Chapel, theaters, museums, churches, schools, and NAACP chapters across the country.

The premier production was directed by Kevin Willmott; designed by Mike Wood; and produced by Scott Richardson. The executive producer was Oz Scott. Musical performers were: Kelley Hunt, Queen Bey, the Ambassadors for Christ Music Ministry of The Historic Sixteenth Street Baptist Church, Al Berman, and Rick Reed.

The cast was:

CHARLES H. HOUSTON: Roger Aaron Brown
THURGOOD MARSHALL: James McDaniel
CISSY SUYAT: Diane Bulan
GARDNER BISHOP, KENNETH CLARK:
    Harvey Williams
WOODY, OLIVER BROWN: George L. Forbes
ELEANOR TOMPKINS: Lauren Arnold

(Cast Continued)

BARBARA JOHNS: Debra Washington
MRS. GATES, LOUISA HOLT: Jeanne Averill
SARAH BULAH, MOTHER, and LUCINDA TODD
  Yolanda King
REV. MARTIN LUTHER KILSON, MATTHEW
  WHITEHEAD: Frank Dodson
REV. J. A. DE LAINE: Granvile O'Neal
MAN WITH GAS CAN, MR. TOMPKINS: Ric Averill
MC KINLEY BURNETT, SILAS FLEMING: Walter
  Coppage
CHARLES SCOTT, JAMES NABRIT: Jason Hardiman

Now Let Me Fly

Time

1948-54, the period leading up to the *Brown v. Board* decision.

Settings

The office of the Legal Defense Fund, NAACP

A barbershop in Washington D.C.

A school auditorium in Farmville, VA

A church office in Hockessin, DE

A burned-down church in Summerton, SC

A railroad yard in Topeka, KS

Story

Thurgood Marshall needs to decide if he is ready to fly in the face of tradition and argue before the Supreme Court to overturn legalized segregation. When the ghost of his mentor, Charles Houston, visits him, he is stricken with doubt. Houston takes Marshall on a journey, looking in on the men and women working in the grassroots struggle against the legally-enforced separation of the races. Houston and Marshall collect the thumbprints of

7

the ordinary people who become activists in all five of the cases that go to the Supreme Court. Together, the thumbprints form a picture of determination, dignity, and success.

Now Let Me Fly tells the story of the unsung heroes and heroines behind the struggle to end legalized segregation in America.

Language

This play makes use of the language of the period it depicts and non-standard English. The script does make use of some powerful language that might be considered by some to be sensitive or controversial.

Scene 1

Music. Several actors take their places on the stage. Charles Houston, a distinguished gentleman in a fine suit, enters to address the audience.

HOUSTON. And they blame it all on me. Me, Charles Hamilton Houston. As if I started the whole thing, like some John the Baptist squalling in the wilderness. They say I have my thumbprints all over it.

(A large image of a thumbprint is projected.)

Look at that thumbprint. Full of whorls, spirals, and loops, a pattern so wild it looks like the map of a bumblebee's flight. Probably belongs to Thurgood Marshall.

(Visuals of more thumbprints and handprints on cave walls.)

Thumbprints. Handprints. We humans have been taking credit or laying blame with them since we lived in caves. And behind each and every mark, there's someone with a story: "I did it," "I made a difference."

(An actor steps forward and holds up a thumb toward the audience as if pressing it to an inkpad. A thumbprint appears on the screen. A second actor steps forward, repeats the action, then a third. More thumbprints.)

Unique. No two the same. Like people. Quite simple then, is it not? We need to go back and find the right thumbprints. Get the real story about who did what.

(Other actors return to their places.)

(HOUSTON puts his thumb up. No print appears.)

You didn't expect a ghost to make a mark, did you?

Scene 2

HOUSTON. Let me take you back to 1950.

> *(Projected images of signs for separate drinking fountains and theatres; images of ramshackle, dilapidated schools.)*
>
> *(Image of New York in 1950.)*

New York City. The offices of the Legal Defense Fund where our Mr. Marshall is addressing a press conference.

MARSHALL. I promise you the end of segregation in five years and the end of racism in 10! The wall will come down! Questions?

REPORTERS. Mr. Marshall! Mr. Marshall!

> *(MARSHALL nods to one.)*

REPORTER 1. Mr. Marshall, you've made some pretty bold statements for someone who just lost a case. Are you planning to appeal?

MARSHALL. The current law states that Negro children are not fit to go to school with white children. Jim Crow must go! As head of the Legal Defense Fund, I will usher him out the door myself, no matter how many cases it takes.

REPORTER 1. Will you appeal to the Supreme Court?

MARSHALL. I plan to announce that decision in the morning.

REPORTERS. Mr. Marshall!!

MARSHALL. Yes?

REPORTER 2. The Supreme Court clearly established the "separate but equal" doctrine. Isn't it your job to stay within the law?

MARSHALL. "Separate but equal?" Show me the equal!

REPORTER 3. Mr. Marshall! Down in Dixie most people believe that control over schools is a local matter. Going to the Supreme Court would upset the apple cart. What would you say to those who believe in states' rights and gradualism?

MARSHALL. I think 90 years has been plenty gradual.

REPORTER 2. Mr. Marshall, you have the weight of the entire Negro race resting on your shoulders. How do you sleep at night?

MARSHALL. Sleep? There's no time to sleep when we're trying to change the law of the land. Thank you! Thank you!

(REPORTERS exit.)

Scene 3

MARSHALL is left in his office with secretary, CISSY SUYAT.

SUYAT. You know, Boss, you had to lose that case. Now, you can appeal. There'll be a new Supreme Court decision with your thumbprint right smack on it.

MARSHALL. That right?

SUYAT. People will be tearing down those ramshackle old colored schools left and right. This is an opportunity, Boss. We should be celebrating! I think we could use a little music because, as you say, "we stuck our skinny little necks out."

(HE *laughs at her remark.* SHE *walks toward the radio, turns it on. Cab Calloway's "Minnie the Moucher" plays.*)

MARSHALL. A-ha! It's my main man, Cab Caloway!

(HE *sings along.*)

Hi-de-hi-de-hi-de ho! Hi-de-hi-de-hi-di ho!

(HE moves to the music.)

SUYAT. Yessir! Mr. Calloway does get one in the spirit.

MARSHALL.

(HE twirls her around in a little dance.)

Hi-de-hi-de-hi-de-ho. Maybe we can turn it into a slogan. *Hi-de-hi-de-hi-de-ho. No more Jim Crow!*

(HE pauses the dance.)

I went to high school with him, did you know that? In Baltimore. Our school was called Colored High.

SUYAT. Whoa! You went to high school with Cab Caloway? I wonder what were you two like back then?

MARSHALL. Cab, he was a wild and crazy cat, full of the devil.

SUYAT. And you?

MARSHALL. *(joking)* I was meek and humble. Nah! I was rambunctious and defiant.

SUYAT. How defiant? Did you ever get arrested?

MARSHALL. Oh, yeah. I had this job when I was 15, delivering fancy ladies' hats...

SUYAT. You got arrested deliverin' hats?

MARSHALL. Listen up. I was carrying a stack of hatboxes about yo high. I was trying to get on the streetcar and got ahead of a white lady in line. An angry white man grabbed my collar and yanked me right off that streetcar. He called me a bad name, referring to the color of my skin. So, I just turned around and...

(HE makes a fist)

SUYAT. What happened to the hats?

MARSHALL. The hats? Don't you care what happened to me?

SUYAT. You survived to tell the tale. The poor innocent hats, on the other hand...

MARSHALL. I dropped the damn hats. Feathers were flying, fists were flying. A nasty fight broke out and I got arrested.

SUYAT. You were a "bad boy."

MARSHALL. Some people thought so.

SUYAT. Even at school? Did they ever put you in detention?

MARSHALL. Mmmm-hmm. When I acted up at Colored High, they sent me down to the basement with nothin' but a copy of the U.S. Constitution. I memorized the whole thing.

SUYAT. So, something good came out of something bad. Just like this case.

MARSHALL. I was just forgetting about the damn case! I lost the damn case.

SUYAT. But you and Mr. Caloway memorized the whole Constitution…

MARSHALL. Well, I did. Cab, he started goin' to night clubs and I started goin' to debate club. I decided I wanted to become a lawyer.

SUYAT. And the people are happy that you did. Mr. Marshall, sir, you are a terrific lawyer. You just need to read your fan mail! Lookee here…

(*SHE looks through a stack of mail, picks up a letter, reads.*)

17

"Dear Mr. Marshall, you are the Number One Negro of All Time. Thank you for trying to make our lives a little bit better. We know you're going to do right by us." There are hundreds of them writing to you, Mr. Marshall. Porters, teachers, garage mechanics. They are all counting on you...

MARSHALL. Do you know what that feels like? When I am out there on the road, speaking in some church basement and I see those hungry faces looking up at me, I wonder what if... What if...?

SUYAT. What if...?

MARSHALL. What if I bluster my way up to the Supreme Court and fall flat on my black bottom? What if I can't...?

SUYAT. Make the world spin the other way?

MARSHALL. Is that what I'm trying to do?

SUYAT. Oh, yes. And please, please, sir, don't you stop trying.

(*SHE moves to leave, waves.*)

Good night, Mr. Marshall.

Scene 4

MARSHALL, left alone, anxious, paces.

MARSHALL. Make the world spin the other way... Or die tryin'!

(HE calls out.)

Charlie Houston! It's all your fault! Charles "Cement Pants!" Houston!! You started this and then you up and left me behind. "Old Iron Shoes," wherever you are, you listen here! I'm gonna take this case all the way to the Supreme Court? Understand? You were my teacher, my advisor. Why aren't you here?! Charlie Houston, you old ghost! Where are you?!

HOUSTON. *(appears)* Mr. Marshall, you are making enough racket to wake the dead!

MARSHALL. Is it really you? Are you a...

HOUSTON. A ghost? Would it help if I said "Boo?" Booooooo!! Are you afraid me yet?

MARSHALL. Hardly.

HOUSTON. That's too bad. Now what is all this racket? I may be dead but I'm not deaf. You could have called in a reasonable tone. I would have come just the same.

MARSHALL. You came because you wanted to. Because you don't trust me.

HOUSTON. And yet, I left you in charge.

MARSHALL. That's right. You're not the boss man around here anymore.

HOUSTON. I can see that. This place is in total disorder. My chair belongs here. The files there. My briefcase is nowhere to be seen. And behold: a radio! In an office of the law!?

MARSHALL. I know why you're here. You don't want me to appeal. You want me stick with the local cases. You don't want me to take a chance on the Supreme Court.

HOUSTON. It's true I used to think we could force the issue of "separate but equal." Try all the local cases. Make them build equal Negro schools. Because it's impossible! They'd have to let the Negro children in the white schools or go broke.

MARSHALL. That's why you came. To preach to me again about gradual change. Well, you had your plan and I have mine.

HOUSTON. I have come for thumbprints.

MARSHALL. Thumbprints?

HOUSTON. And my briefcase, of course. I miss my briefcase.

MARSHALL. Thumbprints?

HOUSTON. In 15th century Persia, it was against the law to draw images. So, people made pictures with thumbprints. I admire their creativity.

MARSHALL. I've got the most important decision of my life to make and you're talking about thumbprints!

> *(HOUSTON extracts his briefcase, seemingly out of thin air.)*

HOUSTON. Change the schools, and you will change the world. We had dreams, didn't we, son?

MARSHALL. I'm not your son. And I still have dreams. I'm gonna win the appeal. *Hi de hi de hi de ho, No mo' Jim Crow.*

HOUSTON. You are not even sure whether you **should** appeal.

MARSHALL. *(doubtful)* I know what I'm going to do. Take this one all the way...

HOUSTON. To the Supreme Court?

MARSHALL. You betcha.

HOUSTON. You want to change the law of the land. Upend the Supreme Court ruling. Reverse gravity.

MARSHALL. You betcha. You don't think I can do it.

HOUSTON. More to the point, **you** don't think you can do it.

MARSHALL. You're my coach. You're supposed to be cheering me on to victory, inspiring me with bits of wisdom.

HOUSTON. *(HE spouts "wisdom.")* Get yourself a good haircut and do not wear white socks in court.

MARSHALL. You really don't think I can do it.

HOUSTON. Mr. Marshall, you—you cannot!

    (MARSHALL deflates.)

For heaven's sake, straighten your shoulders, hold your chin up.

MARSHALL. You didn't do it in your lifetime, so you don't want me to do it in mine?

HOUSTON. My God, man, do you think I am that selfish? I want what is best for our people.

MARSHALL. I'm just starting to fly and you want to clip my wings.

HOUSTON. Do not fly too near the sun!

MARSHALL. What, you think I'm some kinda Black Icarus?
HOUSTON. Heed the warning.

MARSHALL. I don't need a warning.

HOUSTON. Listen to the stories, Mr. Marshall. A lawyer always listens to the stories. Go back to the beginnings. Icarus had a father, Daedalus.

MARSHALL. Dead-less, like you.

HOUSTON. An inventor.

MARSHALL. I know the story. Daedalus and Icarus were imprisoned behind gigantic walls. They could not climb over or dig under them.

HOUSTON. So Daedalus made them…

MARSHALL. Wings. Big beautiful wings for himself and his boy Icarus.

HOUSTON. Wings made of feathers and wax and string. They put on those wings…

MARSHALL. And flappity-fly, they took off. Right over those prison walls.

HOUSTON. Daedalus warned Icarus: "Do not fly too near the sun, for the wax in your wings could melt and you could fall into the sea."

MARSHALL. But Icarus, he was soaring so high, having the time of his life, so proud and happy with those wings his daddy made him, glidin' and soarin', soarin' and glidin', feelin' so good, SOARRRIN'!!

HOUSTON. Until he flew too near the sun. The wax in his wings melted and he fell into the sea.

(Projected images of Daedalus and Icarus.)

MARSHALL. You sure know how to ruin a party.

HOUSTON. Mr. Marshall, you have been flapping your wings and you have been flying high. Now you had better take pause and…

MARSHALL. And do what?

HOUSTON. Do what I taught you. Know every case. Know the people who brought them. Their lives are in your hands. Thank every bird whose feathers are in your wings. Love each bee for every bit of wax.

MARSHALL. I hereby thank you for having the brilliant idea of de-segregating the schools. You were right. If we bring up our children together, it will be the end of racism.

HOUSTON. I'm not talking about me.

MARSHALL. What, you want me keepin' in mind every dishwasher who sent a dime to the NAACP? I'm a lawyer. If I get stuck in the stories of every soldier in the struggle, I can't do my job.

25

HOUSTON. Is that right?

MARSHALL. I'm designing a new society. I can't be arguing before the Supreme Court and still have time to write thank-you notes to every mama who made fried chicken for the cause.

HOUSTON. If you are changing more than the law, if indeed you are changing society, if you are ending racism, you need every mama who made fried chicken for the cause!

MARSHALL. I don't have time for this.

HOUSTON. Gotta fly?

>*(with his hand, HOUSTON mimes flying, then falling)*

MARSHALL. If you weren't such an old man…

HOUSTON. Supernatural being. Ghost. Are you afraid of me yet? Just a touch of the heebie-jeebies?

MARSHALL. Yes! Happy?

HOUSTON. Good.

MARSHALL. What now?

HOUSTON. A good lawyer listens to the stories. Goes back to the beginnings. Gathers thumbprints. Listens to the peoples' blues.

(HOUSTON takes MARSHALL aside to observe.)

Scene 5

Projected image of a 1940s barbershop.

HOUSTON. Washington, D.C., U Street. The barbershop of Mr. Gardner Bishop.

> *(HOUSTON turns on the radio. The blues are playing.)*

> *(WOODY, a veteran wearing an army uniform, sits down to get his hair trimmed. BISH shakes out a towel, ready to cut hair.)*

BISH. What can I do for our hero today?

WOODY. No hero, just a regular soldier. And you can start by turnin' that radio around. I don't like them blues rubbin' off on me.

> *(BISH moves radio.)*

BISH. "Unsung hero," I'd say.

WOODY. I didn't do nothin'.

BISH. You fought Hitler. He was mowin' down everybody who didn't have blond hair and blue eyes and then you...

(HE is distracted by something outside.)

WOODY. You gonna cut my hair or stare out the window?

BISH. Sign across the street. On that new Capital Cafe.

(WOODY rises to look. HE reads.)

WOODY. "White gentlemen and ladies only." They ain't gonna get much bizness here on U Street. Only colored over here.

(BISH continues reading.)

BISH. "**Dogs** belonging to the **appropriate** persons also welcome, **if on a leash.**" They let you in the war to get shot at. They let you in the mine fields. Now you cain't go in a restaurant they let a rat terrier in.

WOODY. Same old, same old. What get into you today?

BISH. (*clips a while, then...*) Didn't you tell me they wouldn't let you in the movies when you was a guard over them prisoners-of-war?

WOODY. Yeah, them Nazi P.O.W.s was inside laughin' it up at Laurel and Hardy and us colored soldiers had to stand outside and shuffle.

BISH. Or how about that time that white soldier thought you was the devil.

(WOODY stands up to demonstrate.)

WOODY. That man, he was lookin' at me like this, sidelong-like, lookin' for my devilly tail. Preacher told him we had tails! Same guy thought we had bumps on our heads where our horns used to be!

(WOODY sits back down. BISH rubs WOODY's head, joking.)

BISH. There they are! I can feel where your daddy musta cut 'em off.

WOODY. You stop messin' with me.

BISH. You quit fidgetin', Woody, or you **will** look like the devil!

WOODY. I come here to relax and you gettin' me all riled up!

(WOODY picks up newspaper with a purposeful snap.)

(BISH clips a bit.)

BISH. It's right there in that paper. How they complainin' that the brand new white school is only half full. I said, half full.

WOODY. I don't look at that kinda news. Now stop it! You're given me the blues.

BISH. Meanwhile ours is bustin' at the seams. Your boy and my girl, they're goin' to school in shifts, only 3 hours a day.

WOODY. Ain't fair, ain't right, but y'cain't fight City Hall.

BISH. I went to the school board meeting last night.

WOODY. What, are you nuts? *Hello, sirs. I'm an angry Black man and I'm here to put my Negro kids in school with your lily-white children.*

BISH. They didn't give me the time o'day.

WOODY. You just lucky you don't work for nobody 'cause your black fanny would be fired, quick as that.

(WOODY snaps his fingers, picks up newspaper again.)

BISH. I figure there's barber shops all over the country where there's guys like you just noddin' and sayin', "You cain't fight City Hall."

WOODY. That's right.

BISH. Meanwhile, there's more signs goin' up about dogs goin' where we cain't.

WOODY. City Hall wall. Cain't get over it, cain't get around it.

BISH. More white schools half empty and more colored schools crowded to the gills. They can turn **me** away from the movies and the cafes but when it comes to my little girl, when it comes to my Judine and her education...

WOODY. You ain't goin' back to that school board!

BISH. What you do for a livin', Mr. Woody?

WOODY. Taxi dispatcher and you know it.

BISH. What if every Negro taxi dispatcher in the whole U.S.A. sent out all the taxis takin' our colored kids to the white schools. They couldn't stop us. If we all did it. They couldn't stop us.

WOODY. Are you nuts? Where you gettin' these wild ideas?

BISH. Nowheres. Okay, I went to a meetin' and this lawyer, Mr. Houston...

WOODY. I thought you hated them suit-wearin' N-double-A-C-P-ers.

BISH. I told this lawyer how hoppin' mad I was. And he said to me...

WOODY. He said?

BISH. A little less "mad" and a little more "do."

WOODY. I already risked gettin' my butt blown to bits for so-called "freedom." I ain't fightin' no more white folks! I ain't fightin' no more white folks, y'hear?

(Enter ELEANOR, a teenaged white girl, looking for all the world as if she's playing

hide-and-seek and just found her hiding place.)

ELEANOR. Oh. Good morning, mister. Sir. Sirs.

BISH. You lost, miss?

ELEANOR. Not at all, sir, thank you. Just...*(SHE notices where she is.)* wanting a haircut.

> *(WOODY rises to let her sit, shaving cream still on his face.)*

WOODY. Here you go, missy. I don't need to sit no mo'. I can just stand right up. Do me good. Yes'm.

ELEANOR. Thank you kindly, sir. I'll—I'll wait my turn, sir.

> *(SHE paces. BISH pretends to continue working on WOODY.)*

WOODY. Now when my wife get her hair done, she go down to the beauty shop. Maybe your mama's thinkin' you're over at the white woman's beauty shop.

ELEANOR. They don't play the blues in the white beauty shop.

WOODY. Them blues? *(HE points to radio.)*

ELEANOR. I wanna learn to sing like Bessie Smith. If only I could be like her and wear a red spangly dress and sing like I know something about the world!

BISH. Bessie Smith? Our Bessie Smith?

ELEANOR. At John Philip Sousa High, we've got teachers for French and physics but not one to teach me how to sing the blues.

WOODY. Why, missy, I know your school. I been there for a basketball game. And I kinda peeked in the science section.

BISH. Woody's son's got a special interest in science.

ELEANOR. We got more microscopes and butterfly collections than we got kids. If he likes that kinda thing, you oughta send your son on over.

(MR. TOMPKINS enters.)

MR. TOMPKINS. Eleanor Tompkins, I've been looking all over creation for you. I told you! When I'm out here collecting my rents, you wait in the car!

ELEANOR. But, Daddy, I just wanted to listen!

MR. TOMPKINS. Eleanor, did these men come near you?

ELEANOR. I'm fine. I just wanted to listen!

MR. TOMPKINS. *(to men)* She don't have no sense.

WOODY. Oh, she wasn't botherin' us none.

MR. TOMPKINS. And looks like you don't have no sense neither, keepin' her in here like that.

ELEANOR. It wasn't like that, Daddy!

WOODY. We just givin' her directions is all. Yessir, uh-huh.

MR. TOMPKINS. *(to men)* My daughter does not need your directions. I own the cafe right across the street. And when I find out who your landlord is, I plan to own this building too, understand?

ELEANOR. Daddy, please!

MR. TOMPKINS. White people built this country and we are gonna take it back if we have to do it block by block.

BISH. Not this particular block because I own this barbershop and I own this building. And it ain't for sale.

MR. TOMPKINS. Ah. One of those uppity Nigroes. Tryin' to take over our schools, our neighborhoods.

WOODY. Don't mind him, sir.

MR. TOMPKINS. Well, let me tell you, Mr. Uppity Negro, white people are in charge because we are smarter, braver, and yes, richer. And by God, we're stayin' in charge. So you can just go back to Mississippi or Africa or wherever you come from. Meanwhile, you leave my daughter alone!

> *(HE pulls ELEANOR outside the shop. Coast is clear.)*

WOODY. We're lucky we didn't get ourselves lynched.

MR. TOMPKINS. *(to ELEANOR)* What were you thinking? You start hangin' around with colored, your own people will start lookin' down on you. Bad enough you're listenin' to that jungle music!

ELEANOR. You can't do this! You can't stop me! Y'know, sometimes I think I was born the wrong color!

MR. TOMPKINS. What?! What?! Little girl, you just thank your lucky stars you weren't born colored!

(HE exits. SHE stands, feeling the blues herself, then, it's like she really hears the blues in her mind for the first time. SHE's more determined. HE comes back, pulls HER off-stage.)

WOODY. Oh, yeah. We lucky to be alive.

(BISH bangs things around.)

You hatin' that girl for walkin' in here like that?

BISH. No, I'm hatin' you for shufflin' around like you some damn Step'n'Fetchit.

WOODY. Never seen anything like it. White girl walkin' in here like she got the right.

BISH. She got the right.

WOODY. And her daddy! Whew!

BISH. And how you expect to be treated any different when you're shufflin' and bowin'?

WOODY. And you think you're helpin' by sassin' him like that! Oh, that's right, you're the one goin' to the school board and creatin' a big fuss, causin' trouble.

BISH. I'm gonna keep on goin' to that school board because schools are where we're gonna change everything.

WOODY. Right. Let me tell you about their schools. They got microscopes, lab tables, charts, scales, beakers. You think they gonna give that up?

BISH. And tell me what kinda science equipment they got over at the colored school? *(No answer.)* It ain't **your** shame, so speak on up!

WOODY. A Bunsen burner and a bowl of goldfish.

BISH. Excuse me?

WOODY. That's all what they got in the whole colored high school. One Bunsen burner and a bowl o' goldfish.

BISH. What our kids gonna learn from watchin' them goldfish swimmin' around? The law of the land is "separate but equal!" Show me the equal! Show me the equal!!

(BISH pounds on a table.)

WOODY. Simmer down, Bish. A little less "mad" and a little more "do."

BISH. I don't care what that NAACP lawyer told me.

WOODY. But he's right. Where's the "do?" What we gonna do?

BISH. I'll give you "do." I'm gonna organize, proselytize, and deputize. We're gonna drive in a parade of taxi cabs to the white school! We'll have a strike, like they do in the unions!

WOODY. You're gonna need a whole lot of customers to carry that off.

(BISH takes down a sign with prices, grabs a pen.)

BISH. Give me your good back, Woody.

(HE writes on the back of the sign.)

We're gonna have us a meetin'. And I'm givin' a speech.

WOODY. You?

BISH. I said I'm givin' a speech!

(WOODY goes toward radio.)

BISH. What you doin', Woody?

WOODY. Just turnin' up the radio. I ain't afraid of them blues no more.

> *(WOODY turns radio up. BISH gives a thumbs-up sign. Blues medley. Projected images of blues singers, then images of children and poverty.)*

Scene 6

HOUSTON waves his hand and thumbprints appear projected on screen.

HOUSTON. Thumbprints, Mr. Marshall. Each one unique. People once used them to sign contracts.

MARSHALL. And I thought you brought me here for a haircut.

HOUSTON. Barbers, cab drivers, housemaids, and teachers all over the country meeting in cafes, truck stops, church basements.

MARSHALL. We got some grassroots people getting together to gripe. It doesn't change the law. What does it have to do with me?

HOUSTON. He was my friend, Gardner Bishop. We worked together organizing protests, talking to people, letting them know they were not alone.

MARSHALL. All the talk does not change the law.

HOUSTON. The law protects us. You throw away the law and what do you have?

MARSHALL. I'm not throwing away the law, I'm changing it.

HOUSTON. We're back to reversing gravity, are we?

MARSHALL. You said it.

HOUSTON. So everything will be flying around. There will be fallout everywhere.

MARSHALL. We'll survive.

HOUSTON. Will we?

MARSHALL. I can feel it in my bones. Here comes The Ghost of Negro Future.

HOUSTON. Is that what you would like?

(HOUSTON waves and images appear of inner-city schools and graffiti.)

MARSHALL. I don't know what you're showing me.

HOUSTON. Schools in the 21st Century.

MARSHALL. I don't believe you.

HOUSTON. Believe me.

MARSHALL. But if we change the law...

HOUSTON. That is the future.

MARSHALL. You're not saying "what goes up must come down." You're not saying that.

HOUSTON. I am saying you have to listen to the stories. Listen to the people.

Scene 7

Projected images of a Farmville, Virginia School.

HOUSTON. Farmville, Virginia. The R. R. Moton High School auditorium. It is the spring of 1950 and a young woman, Barbara Johns, age sixteen, is about to speak. Listen to the people, Mr. Marshall.

(HOUSTON escorts BARBARA JOHNS forward to address a school assembly.)

BARBARA. Every morning I get on a bus thrown away by the white high school. I sit on a torn seat and look out a broken window. And when my bus passes the shiny new bus that the white high schoolers have, I hide my face because I'm embarrassed in my raggedy bus. And when we get to R. R. Moton High, the bus driver gets off with us, because he's also our history teacher. He comes in the classroom and fires up the stove and I sit in my winter coat waiting for the room to get warm. You know

45

the rooms, the ones in the "addition" as they call it. We call them "the tar paper shacks" because that's what they are, am I right? I'm embarrassed that I go to school in tar paper shacks and when it rains I have to open an umbrella so the leaks from the roof won't make the ink run on my paper. And later in the day I have a hygiene class out in that broken-down bus and a biology class in a corner of the auditorium with one microscope for the whole school. I'm embarrassed that our water fountains are broken and our wash basins are broken and it seems our whole school is broken and crowded and poor. And I'm embarrassed. But my embarrassment is nothing compared to my hunger. I'm not talking about my hunger for food. No, I'm hungry for those shiny books they have up at Farmville High. I want the page of the Constitution that is torn out of my social studies book. I want a chance at that "Romeo and Juliet" I've heard about but they tell me I'm not fit to read. Our teachers say we can fly just as high as anyone else. That's what I want to do. Fly just as high. I said, fly. You know, I've been sitting in my embarrassment and my hunger for so long that I forgot about standing up. So, today, I'm going to ask you to stand with me. Before we fly, before we fly just as high as anyone else, we gotta walk just as proud as anyone else. And that's what we're going to do! We're gonna walk out of this school and over to the courthouse. Do you hear me? We're gonna walk with our heads high and go talk to the school board. Are you with me? We're gonna walk out in a strike, yes, I said strike, and we won't come back until we get a real school with a gymnasium and a library and whole books. And we will get them. And it'll be grand. Are you with me? Are we gonna walk? Are we gonna fly?

(BARBARA starts walking and singing.)

("This Little Light of Mine." CHORUS joins in.)

This little light of mine

I'm gonna let it shine

This little light of mine

I'm gonna let it shine

This little light of mine

I'm gonna let it shine

Let it shine, let it shine, let it shine

(BARBARA, as if leading a large group, walks across the stage. MRS. GATES blocks her way.)

BARBARA. As citizens of Prince Edward County, we would like to exercise our prerogative to address the school board.

MRS. GATES. "Prerogative" is a mighty big word, little girl.

BARBARA. My name is...

MRS. GATES. We know who you are. You would be wise to turn tail and head home. I'm sure your grandmother would rather you were in school, not stirring up any trouble.

BARBARA. We have a document to deliver.

MRS. GATES. I wouldn't leave anything in writing if I were you.

BARBARA. To the board of education, ma'am.

MRS. GATES. I am Mrs. Gates, secretary to the judge. I must tell you it would be considerable unwise to leave anything in writing, Barbara Rose.

BARBARA. There are 400 students, ma'am. We are citizens...

MRS. GATES. You are children in over your heads.

BARBARA. We are citizens with a just grievance to voice. We are protected by the Constitution and...

MRS. GATES. *(to students)* Hold your tongues, turn around in an orderly fashion, and return to your classrooms.

BARBARA. No, ma'am.

MRS. GATES. Pardon me?

BARBARA. With all due respect—no, ma'am. We are certain that members of the school board are not aware of the conditions of our school and if only they knew, our grievance would be alleviated. We are citizens.

MRS. GATES. You are children. You have no idea what you are up against. Three hundred years of tradition. I am telling you this for your own good. You walk in there and you are throwing oil on a fire. And trust me, you will be the ones to get burned.

49

BARBARA. We'll take that chance, ma'am. We figure the Farmville jail is too small to hold us all.

MRS. GATES. Jail would be the least of your problems, girl. You walk in there and a plan of action will be set in motion.

BARBARA. Pardon me, ma'am, I don't see how there can be a plan of action. Our assembly was a total secret. We planned it down to a gnat's eyebrow.

MRS. GATES. Even secrets have a way of getting out. You don't want to be starting a second civil war now, do you?

BARBARA. I'm not afraid. I am standing up for my rights and I am not afraid.

MRS. GATES. You are shaking in your Mary Janes and I can see it. Turn around, child!

BARBARA. As a citizen of Prince Edward County...

MRS. GATES. You walk in there, Barbara Rose, and they will close your school. Now isn't it better to have some schooling than none?

BARBARA. They can't do that, ma'am.

MRS. GATES. They **will** do it. They have been talking about it for months.

BARBARA. I cannot believe that, ma'am. Public education is a right!

MRS. GATES. Barbara Rose, you have a responsibility to the children who've followed you. They followed **you.** Are you going to lead them into disaster? They will close your school.

BARBARA. No one would do that. You stop me from being educated, you stop me from being an informed citizen.

MRS. GATES. This is reality, Barbara Rose, not a high school debate. These people don't want you consorting with white children or taking their jobs. Go home or you'll get burned.

BARBARA. We, as citizens of Prince Edward County, would like to exercise our prerogative to address the school board.

VOICE. Let them in, Margaret.

(MRS. GATES steps aside. BARBARA walks in. HOUSTON gives a "thumbs up" sign. He gestures and thumbprints are projected on the screen.)

(CHORUS sings "This Little Light of Mine" as the scene ends.)

Scene 8

Lights up on HOUSTON and MARSHALL.

HOUSTON. The ancient Chinese used to seal their legal documents with warm wax and put their thumbprints on the seal. Nowadays, I'm told, people put their thumbprints on cookies.

MARSHALL. What happens to her? To Barbara Johns?

HOUSTON. She speaks at community meetings, calls our lawyers.

MARSHALL. No, I mean, what happens to **her**?

HOUSTON. Even our lawyers tell the students to go back to school.

MARSHALL. But they don't, do they? And? Don't you hear me, old man, I said, WHAT HAPPENS TO HER?

HOUSTON. Barbara Rose Johns gets sent away to relatives for her safety.

MARSHALL. But then, when the law changes, the colored students will have a good school right? You know what happens, why don't you tell me?

HOUSTON. The public schools in Prince Edward County are closed for five years. Private white academies are set up. Black children are sent away to relatives or...

MARSHALL. Or don't get any education at all? Damn it. Damn it! This girl doesn't fall, like Icarus. She's shot down.

Scene 9

*Projected image of thumbprints
on screen.*

HOUSTON. More stories, more thumbprints, Mr. Marshall. Third stop. Hockessin.

MARSHALL. I know the Delaware cases. Wilmington. Hockessin.

HOUSTON. Mrs. Sarah Bulah goes to visit her church leader.

> *(MRS. SARAH BULAH carries a couple of shopping bags containing eggs and produce to the REV. MARTIN LUTHER KILSON.)*

REV. KILSON. Why, Sarah, I thank you.

MRS. BULAH. I also got for you collard greens picked this mornin', green as grass.

REV. KILSON. Sarah, you do know how to plow God's earth into yieldin' up His gifts. Now what do I owe you for the fruits of your toil?

MRS. BULAH. Reverend, I don't take no money from a man of the cloth and you know it. They is God's gifts and we are happy to share.

REV. KILSON. May God bless you and multiply your bounty.

(SHE doesn't move.)

I look forward to hearing your voice praisin' the Lord come Sunday.

MRS. BULAH. Oh, yes, Reverend, I shall be there.

(SHE doesn't budge.)

REV. KILSON. Fred in good health?

MRS. BULAH. Oh, yes. Fred, Mr. Bulah, he is right fine, thank you.

REV. KILSON. And Shirley Barbara? What is she now, six years old?

MRS. BULAH. You got it on the button, Reverend. You were always good with numbers.

REV. KILSON. I see you drivin' her up the hill here to the school.

MRS. BULAH. It take me a whole hour to walk it! I can't let no six-year-old child climb that hill, oh no.

REV. KILSON. I'm glad you've seen fit to stop all that letter writing to the Governor and what all. I mean, nobody was gonna let Shirley Barbara on that white bus no matter how close it rode near your house.

MRS. BULAH. Thirteen feet, Reverend. Thirteen feet.

REV. KILSON. Did I ever tell you how much I admired what you and Mr. Bulah did takin' in that child?

MRS. BULAH. It's all because of you, Reverend. You're the one who preached it from the pulpit. You talked about that baby girl left abandoned over there in Wilmington. The way you talked about her, it broke my heart. You are such a gifted sermonizer, Reverend. The good Lord done give you the gift of gab.

REV. KILSON. You are flatterin' me, Sarah. I just said the facts. A ten-month-old baby left without milk or parents in that crowded city. But you were the ones who took her in, made her your own child.

MRS. BULAH. Helpless child can't fend for herself. You did the speakin' and we did the doin'. It's the power of your words, Reverend.

REV. KILSON. And you're still takin' good care of her, drivin' her on up the hill to Mrs. Dyson's class.

MRS. BULAH. Mrs. Dyson, she's a good teacher. Sometime, if Shirley Barbara don't understand somethin', why, Mrs. Dyson she come right to the house to teach it to her.

REV. KILSON. We're lucky to have her.

MRS. BULAH. And she got such a hard job, teachin' all them grades in one room like she do. She even takes in the little knee babies—three and four years old. And it ain't like she can send some of them out to play ball like they do at the white school 'cause we ain't got no baseball diamond. And we ain't got those roses to smell like they got over at the white school neither. Just a bunch of dirt and a one-room schoolhouse with one itty toilet next to the closet with the kids' lunches.

REV. KILSON. Sarah?

MRS. BULAH. And pretty much nothin' but dirt. One room and dirt. That's what we got.

REV. KILSON. Mrs. Bulah, why are you here, bringing me twice as many eggs as usual and five times as many collard greens?

MRS. BULAH. Well, you were right about my letters gettin' me nowheres. I writ the Superintendent of Schools and the Congressman.

REV. KILSON. And the Governor.

MRS. BULAH. Three times. They all say the same thing. The state don't transport little Black children in no white school bus even if it pass right smack by your house.

REV. KILSON. As I've told you, Mrs. Bulah, we have to live in peace and harmony with our white neighbors.

MRS. BULAH. So I went and talked to this here lawyer, Mr. Redding? He's the one that won the integration case over at the University. I figured if he could do that, he could do this.

REV. KILSON. Get Shirley Barbara a ride on the white bus? You bothered him with that?

MRS. BULAH. I was mistaken about that, for sure.

REV. KILSON. I should say. Takin' up that busy man's time.

MRS. BULAH. *(butts in)* He wants me to go all the way for complete integration of our public schools here in Hockessin.

REV. KILSON. Pardon me?

MRS. BULAH. He got a case in Wilmington too. We're goin' for the whole state of Delaware.

REV. KILSON. Mrs. Bulah!

MRS. BULAH. And the whole United States of America where we all supposed to be created equal. It's what Mrs. Dyson teach in that little run-down school tho' I don't see how she can make much of a case, lookin' at the white school sittin' acrost from the country club and ours...

REV. KILSON. The law of the land, Mrs. Bulah, is "separate but equal."

MRS. BULAH. I sees lots of separates but not much equals. We know that ain't workin'. So I was thinkin' maybe you could preach about it on Sunday like you did about Shirley Barbara and convince the others to sign on, too, 'cause there's strength in numbers.

REV. KILSON. Sarah, stop! What in tarnation are you jabberin' about? Don't you have the good sense God gave you? What are you tryin' to do, woman? Stir up trouble?

MRS. BULAH. Mr. Redding is goin' to court and get us colored folks a piece of the action.

REV. KILSON. A piece of the action?

MRS. BULAH. Equal education for our children. Mrs. Dyson is the best there is, but she works too hard for too little and don't even have a decent classroom.

REV. KILSON. If you succeed, Mrs. Dyson will be out of a job. You think they're going to let a Black woman teach white children? They will fire her Black self as quick as that.

(HE snaps his finger)

And what's going to happen to the parents who sign your letter? They will be accused of Communism and lose their jobs at the mill. Those children you're so fond of are going to starve if their daddies can't get no work! Have you talked to your neighbors? Have you asked **them** to sign your letter?

MRS. BULAH. Yes, Reverend, I have.

REV. KILSON. And?

MRS. BULAH. Otis say he don't got no kids so he don't care. Martin Shoe can't sign his own name and his wife Marian won't sign it for him 'cause she's afraid the KKK'll git 'em. And the rest is likewise. So scared they don't even wanna buy eggs from me no more.

REV. KILSON. So why did you come to me if the entire congregation is against this?

MRS. BULAH. 'Cause I heard of preachers speakin' out from the pulpit about the struggle. They is like Moses leadin' their people to the Promised Land. I thought about how you led us to Shirley Barbara and I thought if anybody could speak up a storm about what is right for the forgotten children it is you, Reverend Kilson. You gotta tell 'em it's worth the sacrificin' for the good of the future. They'd listen to you.

REV. KILSON. When I talked to the congregation about that abandoned little Negro girl, I believed every word I said. About takin' care of our own. About raisin' up our little children as a community.

MRS. BULAH. It's the same thing.

REV. KILSON. No, Mrs. Bulah, it is not. I am in favor of segregation. I am a man of peace and I believe we must live alongside our neighbors in harmony. I have heard enough about agitated Negroes joining organizations!

MRS. BULAH. You mean the N double A...

REV. KILSON. Spells trouble. We will leave well enough alone.

MRS. BULAH. What you are sayin' is that our colored children, my little Shirley Barbara and the rest ain't good enough to go to that nice school with the roses? They don't deserve it? Good Lord made them of cheaper cloth or somethin'? Isn't that what we sayin' when we quiet about this? I ain't gonna say it no more. God did not make the Negro child out of a cheaper cloth. I will not say it. I'm leavin' now, Reverend. It is clear to me you have less pluck than the chickens in my yard.

(SHE turns to exit.)

REV. KILSON. Mrs. Bulah! I imagine you'll be wanting your eggs back.

MRS. BULAH. You're welcome to my greens and hens' eggs any time, Reverend. But I reckon from now on you'll be shoppin' in town, buyin' them white eggs.

(SHE exits.)

(HOUSTON gestures and thumbprints are added on the screen.)

Scene 10

Lights up on HOUSTON and MARSHALL.
A few feathers are now sticking out of HOUSTON's briefcase.

MARSHALL. That's right, whatever you're doing with those thumbprints, hers belong up there. I like her pluck but...

HOUSTON. The Reverend?

MARSHALL. He scares me. I don't get why our own people quit on us like that.

HOUSTON. Perhaps Reverend Kilson is afraid of ruffling feathers.

MARSHALL. He let her down. He let his whole community down. If he goes on the way he does, he'll stay downtrodden. Under-served and under-privileged.

HOUSTON. Maybe he is afraid of what the future might bring.

MARSHALL. The future? Without racism we could have more architects, problem solvers, city planners.

HOUSTON. Mr. Marshall, Black or white, we are all comforted by tradition, the way things have been. Family, community.

MARSHALL. That little girl in Virginia could take a chance. "Try to fly a little higher," like she said. Why not him, a preacher, a leader?!

HOUSTON. He might have a clearer view of the risks. That somebody could get hurt.

MARSHALL. You're defending him?

HOUSTON. I think you need to know what you are up against.

MARSHALL. You can't defend him! Not you! You're the one who always said, "A lawyer who is not a social architect..."

HOUSTON. "...is a social parasite?" I know what I said.

MARSHALL. You were my role model, my teacher! Now you're trying to scare me?

HOUSTON. You need to stop and think, Mr. Marshall.

MARSHALL. Are you worried about me? Don't. Don't you worry about me fallin' down, old man. You think you gave me wings of wax and feathers? You gave me wings of steel.

HOUSTON. I gave you wings of paper.

MARSHALL. Wings of paper? Yes, the law has wings of paper—it flies!

HOUSTON. I did what I could. I taught you what I knew.

MARSHALL. "Change the schools and you'll change the world." You did teach me that, and then? Then, what happened?

HOUSTON. It was time to pass on the baton. I left you in charge. I had to...

MARSHALL. Leave? Quit? You quit! The N-double-A-C-P, the Legal Defense Fund, me.

HOUSTON. I left you in charge.

MARSHALL. As if that wasn't bad enough, then you had to go ahead and...

HOUSTON. And what?

MARSHALL. You could have lasted us a little longer.

HOUSTON. You think I chose my ending?

MARSHALL. You had to go all the way and...

HOUSTON. *(interrupts)* Was my death a little inconvenient for you?

MARSHALL. You dragged me into this integration business and then, when the going got rough, you...

HOUSTON. *(rushes in)* Went out of my way to make life hard for you?

MARSHALL. You left me behind.

HOUSTON. I left you in charge. I taught you everything I knew and then I left you in charge. An able-bodied, clear-thinking...

(THEY overlap each other.)

MARSHALL. Hard-drinking, philandering...

HOUSTON. Well-educated...

MARSHALL. Foolish, procrastinating...

HOUSTON. Brilliant, insightful...

MARSHALL. Terrified child!

HOUSTON. Look at me, son! I'm here. You called me and I came.

MARSHALL. I didn't call you!

HOUSTON. You summoned me.

MARSHALL. No! It's you. You're. Haunting. Me. Like it or not, your thumbprints are all over this case. Your thumbprints are all over me.

HOUSTON. We're not finished.

MARSHALL. What's wrong with wings of paper?

HOUSTON. They can burn!

Scene 11

Projected image of a church organ.

HOUSTON. Summerton, South Carolina. Look, Thurgood! These people are meeting in their burned-down church! There's a mother with her little boy.

REV. DELAINE. Welcome, Brothers and Sisters.

(Projected image of a preacher.)

MARSHALL. *(to HOUSTON)* That's Reverend DeLaine. I know these people!

REV. DELAINE. Every Sunday, I stand before you and entreat you to praise God. I ask you to call out your Amens, to pat your feet, to lift your voices, to make a joyful noise unto the Lord. This Sunday is no different. God's house is not four walls and a floor but a people. A community of faith and trust and love. Let the Lord hear our voice, our hearts, and our prayer.

CONGREGATION. Amen!

MARSHALL. Amen! *(to HOUSTON)* I know these people. This is my case!

REV. DELAINE. *"Thus saith the Lord, Let my people go."* Exodus, Chapter 8. Lord, our children walked seven miles to the shanty they call a school and now, since the flood, they have rowed boats to school. We asked for a bus and were refused. We signed a petition for a better school. We knew there would be consequences, Lord. Yes. When your servant Harry Briggs signed the petition and his cow was put in jail for trespassing, we laughed a little, Lord.

MARSHALL. *(to HOUSTON)* They said his cow stepped on some headstones in the white graveyard.

REV. DELAINE. We laughed a little less when his employer fired him from his job at the filling station. On Christmas Eve, Lord. When your servant Annie Gibson signed the petition because there were no desks in the school, she lost her job as a chambermaid. And then she lost her land. We have lost our credit. We have lost our jobs. We have lost our land. They have burned our homes to the ground and our church to ashes. They have sent us into exile.

"And the Lord said, I have surely seen the affliction of my people ...and I have heard their cry." Exodus, Chapter 7.

Today we have returned for one more meeting, Lord. This country of ours that preaches freedom, practices the racism of Nazi Germany. This land that extols equality, practices the separatism of South Africa. And there is no equality in enforced separatism and there is no freedom in racism. *(beat)* Lord, we are weak human beings. We have been frightened by the thunder. We have been burned by the lightning. We have nearly drowned in the flood waters of the storm. But we are not beaten. We know that on the other side of the storm there is a brighter day.

A day of hope and equality and freedom.

MARSHALL & OTHERS. Amen!

REV. DELAINE. For now, if there be thunder, we are the Children of Thunder! If there is lightning, we be its Brothers and Sisters! We will make friends of the Storm. We will weather the struggle for the sake of a brighter day for our children and our children's children! For that day, Lord. For their sake.

(A member of the CONGREGATION begins singing a spiritual, "The Lord Will Make a Way Somehow." OTHERS join in. THEY exit or move to the background.)

HOUSTON. Look, Thurgood, the boy has left his mother's side.

(A drunken white man wanders on, carrying a gasoline can and talking to himself.)

MARSHALL. He's got company.

(There is no child actor on stage, only in the visual. Through his actions, The MAN creates the reality of the child.)

MAN WITH A GASOLINE CAN. So she says, "Go, get gas. Move it!" Why cain't she do it her own self, walk down the road a piece? "Move it!" Who does she think I am, her slave boy? Who does she think I am?

(HE spots boy on side of road.)

Well, lookie here what we got on the side of the road. A little pickininny. Don't worry, boy, I'm just lookin' for a little help. I'm wonderin' if you might could point me in the direction of a gas station.

73

*(The MAN looks in the direction the child
has pointed.)*

Lookie, you did me a favor and I got a shiny penny for
you.

*(HE searches in his pockets and pulls out
a penny.)*

See. Only one more thing I wanna know. Is that your
church down the road? The one all burnt to a crisp? The
insane Reverend Delaine's church? I wanna 'splain
somethin' to ya. He ain't preachin' to you right. Unh-unh.
See, if you look up in the sky, you don't see the buzzards
and the crows mixin' together, do ya? Answer me, boy,
do ya? And here on the ground, you don't see the cats
and dogs mixin' together. It's a law of nature, boy. Birds
of a feather.

(HE drops the penny.)

There. See. That's for you. I ain't such a bad white
person. I done give you a penny. Go ahead an' pick it up.
Don't you want the penny? Buy yourself a little penny
candy at the store?

(The MAN watches as the child retrieves the penny.)

(THE MAN steps on the child's hand with his boot.)

MARSHALL. Oh, no.

MAN WITH A GASOLINE CAN. I just remembered. They don't let no little pickininnies in that store, now do they? I wonder why's that? 'Cause yer out here pollutin' the ditch with yer water, pissin' yer nigger water on the side of the road, arencha, boy?

(HE kicks up with his foot, pushing the child to the ground.)

You niggers are causin' all kinds of trouble. The insane Reverend Delaine.

(HE gives another nudge with his boot.)

MARSHALL. Stop it!

HOUSTON. He can't hear you.

MAN WITH A GASOLINE CAN. Turnin' everythin' upside down. I'll show you the way it's supposed to be.

(HE kicks again and again.)

Damn niggers.

MARSHALL. No! Stop it!

(MARSHALL moves toward MAN. HE is stopped by HOUSTON.)

HOUSTON. You can't stop him.

MAN WITH A GASOLINE CAN. Damn niggers.

(HE kicks the child repeatedly.)

Nigger. Nigger. NIGGER!!

(HE kicks until the child lies motionless on the ground. The MAN crumbles and weeps, then HE runs.)

(The child's MOTHER comes out looking for him.)

(When SHE finds him, SHE throws herself on him and wails.)

MOTHER. Noooooo!

MARSHALL. Noooooo!

(Music: "Sometimes I Feel Like a Motherless Child")

(The spoken lines of MARSHALL and HOUSTON alternate with the sung lines of the song.)

SINGER. *Sometimes I feel like a motherless child*

HOUSTON. She cannot see you.

SINGER. *Sometimes I feel like a motherless child*

MARSHALL. What can I do?

SINGER. *Sometimes I feel like a motherless child*

(The CONGREGANTS help the MOTHER up. THEY carry the child off.)

(REV. DELAINE and OTHERS also exit.)

SINGER. *A long way from home*
A long long way from home

MARSHALL. What can I DO??!!

SINGER. *Sometimes I feel like I wish I could fly*

MARSHALL. I'm so tired. So tired of trying to save the white man's soul.

SINGER. *Like a bird up in the sky*

HOUSTON. Is that what you're trying to do? Save the white man's soul?

SINGER. *Sometimes I feel like I wish I could fly*

HOUSTON. It seems like you were feeling for your people.

SINGER. *Like a bird in the sky*

MARSHALL. Of course, I feel for my people!

HOUSTON. Of course.

SINGER. *A little closer to home*

A little closer to home

MARSHALL. And what about the boy? The boy, kicked senseless?

SINGER. *Sometimes I feel like freedom is near*

HOUSTON. The child will die.

SINGER. *Sometimes I feel like freedom is near*

MARSHALL. God, is there any justice?!

SINGER. *Sometimes I feel like freedom is near*

But we're so far away

But we're so so far away

    (Music ends.)

HOUSTON. And you wonder why I am not resting in peace.

MARSHALL. I knew there would be costs but I tried not to think about—a child!

HOUSTON. I blame myself. When I was walking this earth, I should have thought more about the people, Thurgood. Been softer, warmer, more human.

MARSHALL. You were who we needed you to be. Our leader, our father. We needed you to be firm and strong.

HOUSTON. Me, the "Moses" of the movement! I led them into working for a better day, into making sacrifices for the sake of the law. These people gave their jobs, their land, their children for something I started. Something I engineered. You said it yourself: my thumbprints are all over this!

MARSHALL. And what am I supposed to do? How do I go on knowing these people are getting burned and beaten?

HOUSTON. There are reasons to continue.

MARSHALL. You expect me to go on? I dreamed of a future that was free and equal and it does not happen. Segregation persists, racism triumphs. You showed me the future. There is no happy ending. *"Hi de hi de hi de ho, No' mo' Jim Crow."* It doesn't happen. This child died for nothing!

HOUSTON. There are reasons to continue.

MARSHALL. Oh, yeah? Fifty years from now, what will they be saying? That I didn't do my job?

HOUSTON. That isn't the point!

MARSHALL. It is the point. I die a miserable failed old man, singing *"Hi de hi de hi de ho"* in the gutter, is that it?

HOUSTON. You? This is not about you. **You** go on.

MARSHALL. I go on. Tell me.

HOUSTON. To become a judge.

MARSHALL. A judge?

HOUSTON. Circuit judge. Solicitor General. Supreme Court Justice. Satisfied?

MARSHALL. What?

HOUSTON. You go on to serve as a judge on the highest court of the land. Happy?

MARSHALL. You're telling me...something...worked?

HOUSTON. All you care about is your own success? That you made it to the top of your profession?

MARSHALL. A Negro on the Supreme Court. You said a Negro on the Supreme Court.

Answer me this: in 50 years, if I win the case, are there any Black children in the white schools?

HOUSTON. Yes.

MARSHALL. Are there any Black congressmen, governors?

HOUSTON. A few.

MARSHALL. Next thing you'll be telling me that a Black man is going to run for president!

Marcia Cebulska

(HOUSTON, smiles, is notably silent on this one.)

MARSHALL. Are there separate drinking fountains for Black and white?

HOUSTON. No.

MARSHALL. Separate hotels, restaurants, trains?

HOUSTON. Integrated.

MARSHALL. So, there's progress.

HOUSTON. It is not perfect, but there is progress. If you win the case.

MARSHALL. I am supposed to be measuring the cause against a child's life? I CAN'T! I CANNOT DO IT!!

Scene 12

Projected image of Topeka, Kansas.

HOUSTON. Topeka, Kansas. The Santa Fe Railroad yards.

(Projected image of railroad yards.)

MARSHALL. I can't do it. I quit!

HOUSTON. Attorney Charles Scott pays a visit to McKinley Burnett, president of the Topeka NAACP.

(SCOTT & BURNETT enter.)

MARSHALL. No use in doing this.

SCOTT. *(as if finishing his phrase)* My mind is made up.

(MARSHALL backs off and watches.)

BURNETT. What? Charles Scott, what you doing here?

(SCOTT hands him a paper sack with lunch.)

SCOTT. We gotta talk.

BURNETT. You want to get me fired? This isn't a NAACP meeting. This is my job. Over here, I'm a carpenter, a worker ant, get it?

SCOTT. There won't be a case.

BURNETT. What? Why?

SCOTT. Plaintiffs are running scared. People are losing their jobs, getting shot at, their churches torched, their houses burned!

BURNETT. In South Carolina, not Kansas.

SCOTT. It's happening.

BURNETT. We're asking people to go into clean civilized schools and register. We're asking them to go into clean civilized courtrooms and testify.

SCOTT. We are asking them to stick their skinny little necks out.

BURNETT. Like I said, this is Kansas, not South Carolina.

SCOTT. Like I said, it's not gonna work.

BURNETT. I did not put in years of planning, petitioning, and canvassing to quit now.

SCOTT. And what good did it do us?

BURNETT. Our people have been waiting for hundreds of years for freedom. I put in a few hours.

SCOTT. A few hundred hours. And our children are still going to separate schools, treated like second class citizens!

BURNETT. That's why we have to keep on trying.

SCOTT. It's August, it's hot. People just want to sit in the shade of the park and listen to that John Philip Sousa music. It seems like they care more about ice cream than they do their civil rights.

BURNETT. There are times when I care more about ice cream than my civil rights.

SCOTT. I got holes in the bottoms of my shoes from walkin' all over Tennessee Town. I said I would do this if there were a dozen plaintiffs willing to stand up and be counted. I'm here to tell you we are down to the wire and we don't have a dozen people willing to take the chance!

BURNETT. We'll find them. We are asking them to go to civilized schools...

SCOTT. We are asking them to have their names in the newspapers, to be noticed, threatened. For what? We don't even know if it'll work. We stand up and what happens? The schools could get closed. The teachers could get fired.

BURNETT. We'll keep trying 'til we get it right! You and me, we are the architects. We've drawn up plans and now we have to put them into action.

SCOTT. Architects can't do a damn bit of good without carpenters

BURNETT. We'll get them.

SCOTT. People are running scared and I don't blame them.

BURNETT. Then we'll have to draft our friends. Lucinda Todd!

SCOTT. That woman's canvassed, organized meetings, sat down in segregated movie theatres. She's done her part.

BURNETT. Ask her. And your friend who works here, that welder you went to school with—Brown.

SCOTT. Ollie Brown? He's got two little girls to worry about!

BURNETT. Ask him.

SCOTT. And a third child on the way.

BURNETT. That's why he **should** do it.

SCOTT. It's a lot to risk.

BURNETT. Maybe we should let people make up their own minds.

SCOTT. But what if...? What if something happens.

(Pause while BURNETT thinks.)

BURNETT. Where did you get this sandwich, Charlie?

SCOTT. Cafe around the corner.

BURNETT. They handed it to you out the back door, right? You had to stand and wait out by the garbage cans like a beggin' dog to get me this sandwich, right?

SCOTT. So what's new?

BURNETT. And you are an educated man of the law. An intelligent person loaded with talent. You ought to be able to walk in the front door like a human being! Let's not quit now!

SCOTT. Like you've said, generals can't fight without foot soldiers. You tell me I can't do it alone. Well, I'm ready to do my part but where are the foot soldiers? There's trouble out there. Who's going to stand up to it? Who is going to stand up to it?

Scene 13

*Lights up on MARSHALL and
HOUSTON.*

MARSHALL. He's right! Who's gonna stand up now? If I can't go on, how can I ask anyone else?

HOUSTON. Thurgood, that child died because of ignorance. Because of prejudice, because of things you are trying to change. Our people were suffering long before this. Our children are suffering even if you never take the case to court. You know that. You came along and gave the people hope. You gave them strength and courage and backbone. You can give them dignity in their suffering.

MARSHALL. But if I stop, maybe a job will be saved, a life!

HOUSTON. You think you are that powerful? The train is moving with or without you. The people are already taking the risk. Give them the protection of the law. It is what you can do. Give them the dignity of the law. Do what you need to do. Do what I failed to do.

MARSHALL. And what if I try? Who's going to stand up with me? They're talking in schoolrooms and barbershops. That doesn't mean they'll stand up in court. We need experts, lawyers, plaintiffs. Who's gonna stand up now?

Scene 14

Projected image of thumbprints.

HOUSTON. Look to the thumbprints! Look to the people of Topeka, Kansas.

> *(A light comes up on LUCINDA TODD,*
> *dressed in her Sunday best.)*

LUCINDA TODD. My name is Lucinda Todd of Topeka, Kansas. I live in this district. I'm here to register my child for school.

ANOTHER PLAINTIFF. My name is Mrs. Richard Lawton and I live in this district. I'm here to register my child for school.

MORE PLAINTIFFS.

> *(Standing up, speaking as a chorus.)*

My name is Vivian Scales. My name is Mrs. Andrew Henderson, my name is Lena Carper, Shirley Hodison, Darlene Brown.

MORE PLAINTIFFS.

(Standing up, speaking as a chorus.)

My name is Marguerite Emerson, Sadie Emmanuel, Iona Richardson, Alma Lewis, Shirla Fleming.

(A light comes up on OLIVER BROWN, a well-dressed man.)

OLIVER BROWN. *(speaks alone)* My name is Oliver Brown. I live in this district. I'm here to register my child for school.

ALL PLAINTIFFS. *(more insistent & defiant)*

I'm here to register my child for school.

I'm here to register my child for school!

I'm here to register my child for school!!

HOUSTON. Look at them, Thurgood! The people are marching into the schools, marching into the courts and, against ridicule, derision and threat...

(Projection of civil rights images.)

CHORUS OF VOICES.

(Starting out with solo voices, then a few together, shouting at MARSHALL.)

Go back where you came from! Commie! Pinko! Jew! NIGGER!

HOUSTON. Through it all, Thurgood, your plaintiffs, your witnesses, your attorneys stand up. They're with you, Goody.

Scene 15

Projected image of the exterior of a court-house. The sound of a gavel. Individuals come forward and testify in the various courts around the land.

MATTHEW WHITEHEAD. I am Matthew Whitehead, Professor of Education. Yes, I will tell you what I saw. The chairs sent over from the white school were dilapidated and the children could not sit in them. The tables had holes and cracks.

FREDERIC WERTHAM.

(with slight Austrian-Yiddish accent)

I, Dr. Frederic Wertham, hold the scientific opinion that if a rosebush should produce twelve roses and if only one rose grows, it is not a healthy rosebush.

MATTHEW WHITEHEAD. There was no running water.

FREDERIC WERTHAM. The children we have examined interpret segregation in one way and only one way—they interpret it as punishment

LOUISA HOLT. Louisa Holt, psychologist. The fact that it is enforced, that it is legal, has more importance than the mere fact of segregation by itself

KENNETH CLARK. Kenneth Clark, sociologist. I showed the children of Clarendon County a white doll and a brown doll and asked them to respond, telling me which one was the "nice" doll and which one was the "bad" doll.

LOUISA HOLT. A sense of inferiority must always affect one's motivation for learning since it affects the feeling one has of oneself as a person.

KENNETH CLARK. Three out of every four youngsters, when asked the question, "Which of these dolls is likely to act bad?" picked the brown doll.

LOUISA HOLT. It is not simply skin color...the American tradition...hinges upon a belief of treating people upon their own merits, and...not to reject them on the basis of who their parents are.

JAMES NABRIT. As an attorney, I, James Nabritt, have to say that the basic question here is one of liberty. You either have liberty or you do not. We submit that in this case, in the heart of the nation's capital, in the capital of democracy, the capital of the free world, there is no place for a segregated school system. This country cannot afford it, and the Constitution does not permit it, and the statutes of Congress do not authorize it.

SILAS FLEMING. My name is Silas Fleming. Why am I here? I and my children are craving light—the entire colored race is craving light, and the only way to reach the light is to start our children together in their infancy and they come up together.

JAMES NABRIT. The basic question here is one of liberty.

HOUSTON. *(to MARSHALL)* You have done your part, son. You have brought witnesses, plaintiffs, expert testimony. You've filed your briefs. You have argued before the Supreme Court with eloquence. It's time to finish the job.

Go ahead, son.

(MARSHALL steps forward to address the court.)

MARSHALL. Separate but equal is a legal fiction. There never was and never will be any separate equality. Our Constitution cannot be used to sustain ideologies and practices which we as a people abhor.

Scene 16

*Lights up on HOUSTON and
MARSHALL*

HOUSTON. *(to audience)* You know what happens. Even though you know, you want to see it with your own eyes. You want to see the wings unfurl, you want to hear the cry of the chorus. What happens to thumbprints when there are hundreds, when there are thousands joined together? What becomes of them?

(HOUSTON turns back to MARSHALL.)

They will be announcing the decision soon.

MARSHALL. There's feathers sticking out of your briefcase.

HOUSTON. I've been collecting a few loose ends.

MARSHALL. Loose ends?

HOUSTON. Mrs. Bulah gave me some chicken feathers and I got scissors from Bish. Some wax and string to hold it together from Barbara Johns and Reverend DeLaine.

MARSHALL. You got some plan in mind?

HOUSTON. And yes, of course, blueprints from McKinley Burnett and Charles Scott.

MARSHALL. What are you doing?

HOUSTON. What parents and teachers always do. All the while they are issuing warnings about this and that, at the same time, they are fashioning...well, you know what I am fashioning.

MARSHALL. What you said about the future, fifty years from now...

HOUSTON. They'll have to come up with their own Gardner Bishops and Sarah Bulahs.

MARSHALL. You're not worried anymore?

HOUSTON. Of course, I'm worried. But I hear, sometimes, in a storm, you can fly above the weather.

MARSHALL. But you told me I cannot...

HOUSTON. Cannot. Should not. Not alone!

(HOUSTON turns to MARSHALL, gives him a fatherly blessing.)

And you are not alone. You carry us with you, Goody. All of us!

(Very slowly, MARSHALL moves his arms out to his side, unfurling.)

(OTHERS start quietly singing "Now Let Me Fly.")

(MARSHALL moves his arms straight out.)

HOUSTON. Now listen. Listen to the word of the people, the word of the court.

SUPREME COURT JUSTICE WARREN. We conclude that in the field of public education the doctrine of "separate but equal" has no place. Separate educational facilities are inherently unequal.

HOUSTON. Go ahead, son. We are all doing this with you. Go on now, fly!

(MARSHALL's arms spread out like wings.)

Scene 17

A party at the Legal Defense Fund Offices.
ALL present and cheering.

SUYAT. I told you it would happen, Boss!

MARSHALL. We did it! WAHOO!!!

(MARSHALL twirls CISSY around in a dance. The celebration escalates.)

STAFF. *(chants/sings) Hi de hi de hi de ho, No mo' Jim Crow!*

OTHERS. Speech! Speech! Speech!

(MARSHALL lifts his glass in a toast)

MARSHALL. We gotta give thanks. To Charlie Houston—the Moses of the Movement—we were just following your lead. To all of you—staff, lawyers, plaintiffs—your thumbprints are on this decision! To every dishwasher who gave a dime to the NAACP, and every mama who made fried chicken for the cause, this is for you!

(HE waves decision around.)

We are all gonna fly! We did it! Wahoo!!

(HOUSTON nods to the audience, then, watching from the sidelines, flicks his hand. On the screen, thumbprints accumulate and morph into an image of WINGS! HOUSTON gives a "thumbs-up" sign, waves, exits. Celebratory gospel music; "Now Let Me Fly" and "This Little Light of Mine.")

END OF PLAY

PHOTO COURTESY OF VCU LIBRARIES

ABOUT THE AUTHOR

Marcia Cebulska grew up in Chicago and has spent most of her career writing for the stage and screen. Her critically acclaimed plays have been produced at thousands of venues worldwide and her screenwriting aired on PBS. She has received the Jane Chambers International Award, the Dorothy Silver Award, and several master artist fellowships. Her most recent work includes the guided journal *Skywriting*, her novel *Watching Men Dance*, and her memoir *Lovers, Dreamers, & Thieves*. She lives in Topeka, Kansas with her husband, historian Tom Prasch.

www.marciacebulska.com

Made in the USA
Monee, IL
05 May 2025

16808513R00069